REMEMBERING WORLD WAR I

CAMPAIGNS OF WORLD WAR I

Nick Hunter

Heinemann
LIBRARY
Chicago, Illinois

© 2014 Heinemann Library
an imprint of Capstone Global Library, LLC
Chicago, Illinois

To contact Capstone Global Library please phone 800-747-4992, or visit our website www.capstonepub.com

Edited by Andrew Farrow, Laura Hensley, and John-Paul Wilkins
Designed by Joanna Malivoire and Clare Webber
Original illustrations © Capstone Global Library Ltd 2014
Illustrated by HL Studios
Picture research by Ruth Blair
Production by Sophia Argyris
Originated by Capstone Global Library Ltd
Printed in China by Nordica.   072013   007596R
0813/CA21301399

17 16 15 14 13
10 9 8 7 6 5 4 3 2 1

Library of Congress Cataloging-in-Publication Data
Hunter, Nick.
  Campaigns of World War I / Nick Hunter.
    pages cm.—(Remembering World War I)
  Includes bibliographical references and index.
  ISBN 978-1-4329-8081-8 (hb)—ISBN 978-1-4329-8086-3 (pb)—ISBN 978-1-4846-0100-6 (ss)
1. World War, 1914-1918—Campaigns—Juvenile literature. 2. World War, 1914-1918—Causes—Juvenile literature. I. Title.

 D521.H78 2014
 940.4'1—dc23   2012042717

Acknowledgments
The author and publisher are grateful to the following for permission to reproduce copyright material: AKG Images pp. 4 (Jean-Pierre Verney), 11 (ullstein bild), 17, 20, 27 (Interfoto), 32 (De Agostini Picture Library), 42 (Sites & Photos) 5, 8, 10, 15, 22, 23, 28, 29, 34, 35, 40; Getty Images pp. 6 (Popperfoto), 13, 14, 18, 19, 30, 31, 33, 38, 41 (Hulton Archive), 21 (Interim Archives), 25, 36, 37 (Time & Life Pictures).

Cover photograph of Russian World War I troops with fixed bayonets reproduced with permission of Corbis (© George H. Mewes/National Geographic Society).

We would like to thank John Allen Williams for his invaluable help in the preparation of this book.

Every effort has been made to contact copyright holders of any material reproduced in this book. Any omissions will be rectified in subsequent printings if notice is given to the publisher.

CONTENTS

Some words are shown in bold, **like this**. You can find out what they mean by looking in the glossary.

WHAT WAS WORLD WAR I?

On November 11, 1918, the guns finally fell silent in the most destructive war the world had ever seen. World War I had raged for four years.

The war started in Europe in August 1914. Germany and **Austria-Hungary** faced the combined forces of Great Britain and France in the West, and Russia in the East. The warring countries controlled **empires** and other lands outside Europe, meaning that the war quickly spread to Africa and Asia. World War I became the first truly global conflict, especially when the United States entered the war in 1917.

This division of Senegalese snipers formed part of the French army in 1914.

By the end of the war, around 10 million people had been killed on the battlefield, and millions of **civilians** had also lost their lives. The war caused so much death and destruction that people called it the Great War. They could not imagine another war that could be worse. However, just 20 years later the world was at war again, when World War II broke out in 1939. The Great War was now called the First World War, or World War I.

In Their Own Words

"I think about my family and about all the women of France waking up this morning with a great sense of relief, apart from those left to cry on their own."

French Captain Paul Tuffrau, in his diary for November 12, 1918

World War I in Western Europe was fought around muddy **trenches**, shattered by guns and explosives.

HOW DID THE WAR START?

The final crisis that led to the war happened over just a few weeks. But tension had been building between the great powers of Europe for many years. These powers wanted to dominate Europe and the wider world.

ALLIANCES AND ARMS

Germany had only been a united country since 1871. It came together after a war in which Prussia (a former kingdom of Germany) defeated France and seized the region of Alsace and Lorraine, which poisoned relations with France. The uneasy peace after 1871 was one of the longest in Europe's history. However, Europe's powers began to build **alliances**. This meant that if two countries went to war, other countries would be dragged into the conflict to help their allies.

Warships, **artillery**, and other weapons of war were more destructive than ever before. Countries used their industrial strength to build more and better weapons and warships than their neighbors. This arms race raised the tensions even more.

The HMS *Invincible* was launched at the Armstrong Whitworth Shipyard on the Tyne River in 1907. It was lost in the Battle of Jutland in 1916 (see page 26).

Kaiser Wilhelm II (1859–1941)

Wilhelm II became Germany's emperor in 1888 and ruled until the end of World War I. He was the grandson of Britain's Queen Victoria. Wilhelm wanted Germany to be the most powerful nation in Europe. He ordered the building of a great navy to rival that of Great Britain, which the British saw as a threat to the safety of their homeland. Wilhelm II was forced from power as Germany faced defeat in 1918. He lived in exile in the Netherlands until his death.

COLONIES AND CONFLICT

The decades before 1914 also saw nations trying to show their power around the world. Germany joined Great Britain and France in seizing **colonies** across Africa. In Eastern Europe, Russia and Austria-Hungary tried to wrestle control of parts of Turkey's declining empire. It was here, in the Balkan Mountains of southeastern Europe, that the trigger for war came.

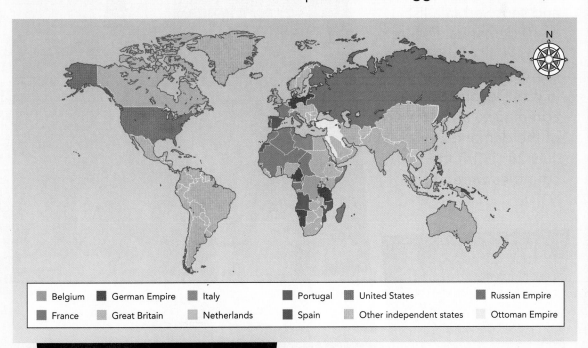

■ Belgium	■ German Empire	■ Italy	■ Portugal	■ United States	■ Russian Empire
■ France	■ Great Britain	■ Netherlands	■ Spain	■ Other independent states	■ Ottoman Empire

European empires controlled many parts of the world in 1914.

ASSASSINATION IN SARAJEVO

Austria-Hungary was a fragile empire in 1914, made up of different regions speaking different languages. Some of these lands wanted to be independent countries. Serbia was becoming more powerful in the region. It was not a good time for the heir to the Austrian throne, Archduke Franz Ferdinand, to travel to Sarajevo on the edge of the empire.

A small group of **terrorists** threw a bomb at his car but missed their target. They thought their plan had failed. However, they got another chance when the car took a wrong turn. Terrorist Gavrilo Princip shot and killed the archduke and his wife.

The terrorists were supported by Serbia. Austria-Hungary decided that Serbia should pay for the murder of Franz Ferdinand. It asked Germany for support and sent Serbia a list of 10 demands. Failure to meet all of these demands would result in war. Despite Serbia agreeing to all but one of the demands, on July 28, 1914, the two countries were at war.

Gavrilo Princip is arrested after shooting Archduke Franz Ferdinand.
A few weeks later the world was at war.

THE SLIDE INTO WAR

The system of alliances meant that this small war swept across Europe. Russia would not allow Austria-Hungary to attack its ally Serbia. When Russian troops began to **mobilize**, Germany supported its ally Austria-Hungary by declaring war on Russia and its ally France. Great Britain declared war on Germany on August 4, after German armies invaded Belgium to reach France. Britain had promised to protect Belgium, which occupied an important strategic position along the English Channel.

In Their Own Words

"I beg you in the name of our old friendship to do what you can to stop your allies from going too far."

Russia's ruler Tsar Nicholas II, in a telegram to his cousin Kaiser Wilhelm II, July 28, 1914

TAKING SIDES

Allied countries in 1914
France, Great Britain, the British Empire (including many troops from India, Australia, Canada), Russia, Serbia, Belgium

Later joined by
Italy (1915), the United States (1917), Romania, Greece, many other countries

Central Powers
Germany, Austria-Hungary, Turkey (from October 1914)

Later joined by
Bulgaria (1915)

WHERE WERE THE WAR'S FIRST BATTLES?

Germany had been planning for war for many years. The German generals knew that they would have to defeat both France and Russia. They planned to defeat France in a few weeks and then move their armies to face the vast armies of Russia, which would take longer to prepare for action.

Powerful, quick-firing artillery was one of the key weapons of World War I.

MOBILIZATION

Across Europe, millions of men were mobilized to fight the war. The German army of 3.5 million soldiers faced a French force of 3 million. Most young men in these countries were expected to serve in the army. Great Britain had only a small force of 150,000 full-time soldiers, although many more volunteered in the first weeks of the war.

In the west, the first battles of the war were fought in Belgium and along the borders between France and Germany. German troops marched through Belgium. The first French attacks were into the land they had lost to Germany in 1871. The French army lost 250,000 men in the first weeks of the war, an early warning of the suffering to come.

The Belgian army was not well equipped to halt the advance of the powerful German army.

In Their Own Words

"In the first days of mobilization there was of course a lot of enthusiasm. Everyone was shouting and wanted to go to the front... The war, we thought, was to last two months, maybe three months."

Robert Poustis, a French student

DEADLOCK IN THE WEST

German forces captured Brussels in Belgium on August 20, and it looked as if they would capture Paris, until they were forced back by French and British resistance. The taxis of Paris were used to carry troops to the front line to defend the city.

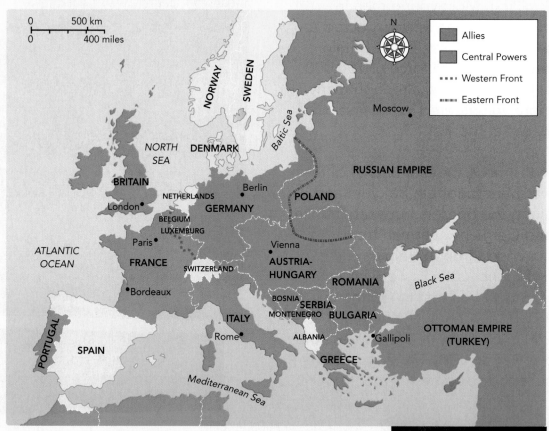

Generals on both sides soon realized that this war would be very different from previous ones. In previous wars, **cavalry** troops on horseback had been able to charge the enemy's guns. In 1914, horses were no match for machine guns, quick-firing artillery, and accurate rifles that could hit a target more than 1 mile (1.5 kilometers) away. Military vehicles in 1914 were not tough enough to be used on the front line, so armies could only move very slowly against powerful defenses.

This map shows the two main front lines of the fighting in Europe. The **Eastern Front** between Russia, Germany, and Austria-Hungary was longer and moved more than the Western Front during the war.

As German troops were pushed back from Paris in the Battle of the Marne, they dug defensive positions called trenches. Gradually, these trenches extended from the English Channel to Switzerland (see map). The network of trenches and the area of fighting around them was known as the **Western Front**. Despite huge efforts and hundreds of thousands of lives being lost, Britain, France, and Germany could not break through these trench lines. The Western Front moved little from the end of 1914 until spring 1918.

In Their Own Words

"While we were watching there was a sound of heavy gunfire and... three heavy explosions. When the smoke had cleared, we saw this group picking up [one soldier] and immediately start to dig a grave for him... That was the first time we realized what the war was about."

Private Clifford Lane of the British army, arriving at the Western Front

British soldiers in the trenches on the Western Front during 1914.

WHAT WAS FIGHTING LIKE ON THE EASTERN FRONT?

As the Western Front became a scene of bloody trench warfare, there were high hopes that Russia would overwhelm Germany and its allies in the East. Russia had a huge population, but the country's industry and armies were less advanced than those of Germany, France, and Great Britain.

The war in the East began with Austria-Hungary's attack on Serbia. The Serbs were fighting for their survival and won some surprising victories. They fought bravely until they were forced into a bitter winter **retreat** into the Albanian mountains in late 1915.

Austrian generals thought victory over the Serbs would be easy, but the Serb forces were well armed and experienced soldiers.

THE RUSSIAN FRONT

The war in the East was fought over a longer front line. This meant that the armies were able to move more. At first, Russia threatened Germany in the East. Then it suffered a humiliating defeat at the Battle of Tannenberg in late August 1914. The Russian armies retreated across Poland and back to the huge open spaces of Russia.

Russia's Cossack cavalry charge into battle in 1914.

WHO'S WHO?

Tsar Nicholas II (1868–1918)

The last tsar (emperor) of Russia had faced unrest from his people for many years before the start of the war. Nicholas had total power in Russia, but lacked the political skills to use it wisely. In 1915, he took personal charge of the Russian army. Defeats in the war caused further unrest and in spring 1917, Nicholas was forced to leave power during a **revolution** in Russia.

DID YOU KNOW?

The Russian army had many more cavalry than other nations. This caused problems because horses need to be fed. Four thousand cavalry soldiers and their horses needed as many supplies as 16,000 **infantry**.

RETREAT AND PRISONERS

During 1915, Germany had a chance to break Russian forces. The Russians were forced back into the vast open spaces of their own country. Although Germany took more than 750,000 Russian prisoners, they could not spare enough forces from fighting on the Western Front to finish off their eastern enemy.

More than half of the war's 8 million prisoners of war were captured on the Eastern Front. Captured soldiers were treated fairly on all sides, but food for prisoners was sent from their home countries. Poor organization and shortages of food at home meant that Russian and Austro-Hungarian prisoners often went hungry.

In Their Own Words

"If someone had said to me, 'One day you're going to eat soup made from dirty potatoes,' or 'You're going to fight over a swede,' I would have said 'What nonsense!'... The hunger is dreadful, you feel it constantly day and night."

Alexei Zyikov, a Russian prisoner of war in Germany, 1916

UNCERTAIN ATTACKS

Russian forces had more success against the weaker armies of Austria-Hungary and Turkey in the south. However, after successful attacks against Austria-Hungary by Russian General Brusilov in 1916, German forces were sent to help their ally Austria. Neither side had the strength for a decisive attack on the Eastern Front.

Sergei Brusilov (1853–1926)

Brusilov was one of the most successful generals of the war. He led a Russian **offensive** in 1916 that seriously weakened the armies of Austria-Hungary. Brusilov's daring, surprise offensive was a contrast to the **stalemate** on the Western Front, where defensive trench systems were well established.

By 1917, the war on the Eastern Front became more like the trench warfare on the Western Front.

HOW DID THE WAR BECOME A WORLD WAR?

Although the largest armies were battling in Europe, the war soon spread to other continents. Japan, Australia, and New Zealand wasted no time in capturing the small German lands and military bases in Asia and the Pacific Ocean. Only the Americas remained largely untouched by the war in 1914. President Wilson pledged that the United States would not get involved in the war.

Thousands of Australian soldiers leave Melbourne to fight in Europe and the Middle East.

DID YOU KNOW?

The British and French armies included many troops from their colonies overseas. British forces included 2.8 million troops from its empire, including 1.4 million Indians.

Soldiers fighting in European countries' African colonies had to deal with very different terrain from the muddy battlefields of Europe. The dense jungle of Germany's colony in Cameroon was eventually captured by troops from British and French colonies in 1916. German East Africa held out against Indian and South African troops until after the war ended in Europe.

A WEAK LINK?

In November 1914, Turkey joined the war on the side of Germany. The **Allies** believed that Turkey was the weakest member of the **Central Powers** and made plans for new attacks away from the trenches of France.

WHO'S
WHO?

Winston Churchill (1874–1965)

Churchill is best known as Great Britain's inspiring leader during World War II. He also played an important part in World War I. He oversaw improvements in technology and the growth of the British navy before the war.
In 1915, he argued for an attack on Turkey to reduce pressure on the Western Front. Later in the war, Churchill became minister for munitions. This meant he was in charge of ensuring there were enough weapons and shells for the army.

THE GALLIPOLI CAMPAIGN

The Dardanelles is a narrow waterway connecting the Mediterranean and Black seas. By capturing the area, Britain and France could attack Turkey and Austria-Hungary from the south and send supplies to their ally Russia.

The first plan was to capture the straits with a naval attack that would destroy Turkish defenses. This plan failed. On April 25, 1915, Australian and New Zealand Army Corps (ANZAC), British, and French troops landed at Gallipoli and Cape Helles to attack Turkish guns and forts. Bad planning and mistakes in the landing meant that the soldiers were unable to advance far from the beaches where they landed. In fierce fighting, they managed to cling to their positions, and the two sides faced each other in trenches much like the Western Front. Another landing of troops in August failed to break the deadlock.

DID YOU KNOW?

On May 24, the two sides called a **truce** to bury the 3,000 dead and decaying bodies in the narrow space between their positions, called No Man's Land. Disease was a major problem for troops in the heat of the Turkish summer.

Turkish defenses were strong enough to hold back the Allied attack on Gallipoli.

RETREAT FROM GALLIPOLI

The Allied leaders had to decide whether to send **reinforcements** or abandon Gallipoli. In the end, after months of heavy losses on both sides, the troops were **evacuated** from the Dardanelles in December 1915. The expedition became a symbol of needless loss of life, and heroic actions by individual soldiers.

An Australian soldier carries a wounded comrade during the Gallipoli campaign.

In Their Own Words

"When we disembarked from our boats on the beach, the conditions were indescribable. There were the wounded, dead, and dying, rifles left all over the place, and the packs the chaps [men] had chucked off when they advanced in the first assault."

Australian Sergeant Frank Kennedy lands at Gallipoli

THE CAMPAIGN IN THE MIDDLE EAST

In 1914, Turkey was struggling to hold on to the huge Ottoman Empire that it had controlled for centuries. The crumbling empire included much of the Middle East.

The Suez Canal in Egypt was a vital waterway. It was essential for transporting troops and supplies from India and Australia to the battlefields of Europe. Allied forces also wanted to protect oil supplies from around the Arabian Gulf, which were needed to power ships and other vehicles. Between 1915 and 1917, the Allies defended these areas and pushed troops into Mesopotamia (modern Iraq) with limited success.

Australian troops riding camels in the Egyptian desert.

PALESTINE

The biggest successes came in Palestine. The Allies were helped by the Arab Revolt against Turkish rule. Arab forces combined with a British army from Egypt to push the Turks northward. In December 1917, they finally seized the important city of Jerusalem. The armies had to fight desert conditions and a lack of water as well as attacking the enemy.

DID YOU KNOW?

There were few roads in the deserts of the Middle East. Horses and mules replaced road transportation. The Allied soldiers and animals needed 400,000 gallons (1.8 million liters) of water every day.

WHO'S WHO?

Lawrence of Arabia (1888–1935)

T. E. Lawrence was studying ancient ruins and making maps for the British army in the Middle East when the war broke out. He helped Prince Faisal bin Hussein lead the Arab Revolt against Turkish rule. Lawrence even took on Arab dress and customs. He was called "Lawrence of Arabia." Lawrence believed that the Arabs should be given full independence after the war, but this did not happen.

WAR IN THE ALPS

Before 1914, Italy had been allied with Germany, but in 1915 the country entered the war on the side of the western Allies. The Italians wanted to grab land from the weakened forces of Austria-Hungary, but they paid a high price.

The only way for Italy to attack its enemy was through the high passes of the Alps Mountains. As the troops climbed, they faced attack from above. In several battles around the Isonzo River between 1915 and 1917, the Italians failed to break through. Badly equipped troops often fought hand-to-hand with clubs.

CAPORETTO

Finally, in August 1917, the Italians broke through the Austrian lines in the 11th Battle of the Isonzo. But this huge effort had almost destroyed the Italian army. Italian soldiers had been very badly treated by their officers, and the mountain fighting had taken a heavy toll. In October 1917, they were defeated by Austrian and German forces in the Battle of Caporetto. Many of the exhausted Italians simply refused to fight. Ten thousand Italians were killed in the battle and almost 300,000 were taken prisoner.

In Their Own Words

"Now and then, in the more difficult passes, someone falls off the edge. They fall without making a sound, as we have been ordered....Artillery shells fly past with a sinister howl; continuous rifle volleys echo from all directions. During each brief stop, exhausted men fall asleep on the ground."

Italian soldier Virgilio Bonamore describes a march into the Alps, July 5, 1915

Italy's Alpini troops led the mountain attacks. They were specially trained for fighting in the ice and rock of the Alps.

WAS THE WAR ONLY FOUGHT ON LAND?

In the years before the war, Germany and Britain competed to build the biggest and most modern warships. When the war came, there were few large naval battles. However, control of the seas was essential because all countries needed to transport supplies and troops across the oceans if they were going to win the war.

In the first months of the war, the British navy targeted German ships to prevent them from leaving their ports in the north of Germany. The British also began a **blockade** to stop merchant ships from reaching Germany. Over the months and years that followed, this blockade led to shortages of food and war supplies.

BATTLE OF JUTLAND

The only time the main British and German fleets of warships met was at the Battle of Jutland in June 1916. The German fleet included more than 100 ships of various sizes, and the British fleet was even bigger when they met off the coast of Denmark. The British lost more ships, but they could claim victory as the German fleet returned to its bases and did not try again to face the British in open battle.

DID YOU KNOW?

The Battle of Jutland involved around 250 ships and 100,000 men. In terms of the **tonnage** of ships engaged, it was the largest battle in naval warfare history. Jutland was also the last of the great battleship battles. Never again did naval battle fleets come together in such large numbers.

In Their Own Words

"There was a terrific explosion,…within half a minute the ship turned right over and she was gone. I was about 180 feet (55 meters) up, you understand, and I was thrown well clear of the ship otherwise I would have been sucked under."

Signalman G. Falmer of the battlecruiser HMS Indefatigable, sunk at the Battle of Jutland

BENEATH THE OCEAN

The most effective weapon at sea in World War I was the submarine. In 1914, the British navy had twice as many submarines as Germany, but it was the German submarines, called U-boats, that had the biggest impact on the war.

German U-boats were the country's main weapon to stop troops and supplies from reaching the western Allies, especially Great Britain. It was a controversial tactic because they sunk many ships from countries not at war, and ships carrying civilians. There was outrage when the liner *Lusitania* was torpedoed in 1915, with 128 Americans among the 1,198 lives lost. This event caused some Americans to reconsider entering the war against Germany.

In 1916, Germany decided to declare war on all shipping heading for Britain. Germany knew that this might bring the United States into the war. It also knew that, if it could not stop supplies from reaching British ports, the Allies would get stronger. Eventually, Germany would be starved into losing the war because of the British blockade.

The tactic nearly worked, with more than a tenth of the world's ships sunk between 1917 and 1918. But the use of **convoys** of ships sailing together helped the Allies win the battle against the U-boats.

There were never more than 60 U-boats at sea at the same time, yet they sunk hundreds of Allied ships.

In Their Own Words

"All the moisture in the air condensed on the steel hull plates...dropping and spraying on your face with every movement of the vessel...It was just like a damp cellar. In one small corner of the central station there was a toilet separated by a curtain."

German U-boat officer Johannes Spiess describes conditions on board

Life on board a U-boat was cramped and difficult.

AIR WAR

World War I was the first war to include aircraft. Most countries had few aircraft at the start of the war. At first, planes were mainly used to gather information about the enemy. Then fighter planes armed with machine guns were built to try to prevent spying from the air.

Most fighter aircraft in World War I were biplanes.

FIGHTER ACES

There were lots of problems with aircraft technology, such as developing machine guns that could fire without damaging the propellers of their own planes. However, the German Fokker aircraft solved many of these problems. In 1916, life expectancy for British pilots in the air was just 11 days. However, by the end of the war, the number of planes produced by the Allies gave them the edge in the battle to control the skies.

Zeppelin airships bombed cities in France and Britain, but these slow-moving bombers were too easy to shoot down. By 1918, aircraft technology had developed to include heavy bombers. This helped to change the war on the front line, and also put cities like London in more danger of attack.

WHO'S WHO?

Baron Manfred von Richthofen (1892–1918)

Von Richthofen, known as the Red Baron, was the most successful fighter pilot of World War I. He came from a wealthy family and was a cavalry officer before becoming commander of Germany's Fighter Wing. Richthofen shot down 80 enemy aircraft before his own final flight in 1918, when he was caught in anti-aircraft fire.

The Fokker Eindecker was one of the first aircraft to use a machine gun that fired between the plane's propeller blades.

HOW WAS THE DEADLOCK BROKEN?

The year 1916 saw some of history's bloodiest battles at Verdun and the Somme on the Western Front. The sacrifice of hundreds of thousands of soldiers failed to move the Front by more than a few miles.

At the start of 1917, mutinies swept through the French trenches as soldiers refused to fight anymore. However, the bloody struggle continued as British and German forces battled in the muddy conditions of the Battle of Passchendaele in summer and fall of 1917.

RUSSIA REVOLTS

In the East, the war changed dramatically. Russians had suffered around 7 million dead and wounded in the war by 1917. The country's people had finally had enough of its uncaring and incompetent rulers. Tsar Nicholas II was forced to step down in March 1917. When a new **communist** government came to power in a revolution in November 1917, it planned to make peace with Germany.

A Russian poster urges workers around the world to join the Russians in rebelling against their leaders and the war.

German soldiers on the Western Front were in desperate need of reinforcements.

With Russia in turmoil, Germany and its allies could bring more forces to the Western Front. They knew their advantage would not last long. The people of Germany and Austria-Hungary were facing severe food shortages. The factories making vehicles and weapons of war were also lacking supplies. They could be overwhelmed by the industrial might of France, Great Britain, and its new ally—the United States.

In Their Own Words

"A Russian officer came over and gave himself up. He told us that whole battles are going on behind their lines. Their officers are shooting at each other and the soldiers are doing the same."

Rudolf Hess, a German soldier, writes to his parents from the Eastern Front, May 19, 1917

THE UNITED STATES AND THE WAR

The United States declared war against Germany on April 6, 1917. President Wilson and the country had tried not to favor either side. Many German-Americans supported the Central Powers, and others did not want to get involved in a European war.

Germany feared the ability of U.S. industry to produce weapons and equipment as much as it feared U.S. soldiers. This was one reason why Germany launched unrestricted submarine warfare in January 1917. Any ships—including U.S. ships—supplying the Allies could be sunk without warning. This would probably have been enough to bring the United States into the war, but the final straw was a message from the German government called the Zimmerman telegram. The telegram urged Mexico to join the war and attack the United States.

U.S. troops leaving home faced a long journey by sea to the battlefields of Europe.

THE U.S. ARMY AT THE FRONT

It was many months before U.S. troops joined the fighting. Only 177,000 soldiers reached Europe by the end of 1917, a small proportion of the millions at the front. The first independent offensive by the U.S. Army was at St. Mihiel on September 12, 1918, where the U.S. troops took 8,000 German prisoners. By the end of the war, the United States had trained and mobilized more than 4 million troops, which made a big difference as the last battles were fought on the Western Front.

American soldiers help seize a town on the Western Front. The U.S. Army began to have a big impact on the war as 250,000 soldiers arrived in Europe each month during the summer of 1918.

DID YOU KNOW?

U.S. troops lifted the spirits of the Allies. During one battle, U.S. Marine Corps Captain Lloyd Williams was urged to retreat. "Retreat? Hell, we just got here," he replied. He did not survive the battle and died a hero.

THE FINAL BATTLES

At the beginning of 1918, few of those fighting would have predicted a quick end to the war. On the Western Front, the front line had barely moved for three years. Morale in many armies was low.

On March 21, Germany launched a ferocious attack on the British army. In a few days, they gained more ground than any attack had managed on the Western Front since 1914. The attacks continued through April and May. Advancing over the craters and barbed wire of the shattered battlefields meant it was very difficult to keep the armies supplied and move the heavy guns.

DID YOU KNOW?

As they stormed British trenches in March 1918, German troops were shocked by the supplies they found. They had been told that the Allies were starving, but they found food that had not been seen in Germany for years.

The first tanks were used by the British army in 1916. These new armored vehicles were important in ending the deadlock on the Western Front.

TURNING THE TIDE

As German forces approached Paris, it seemed as if they might win the war. But Germany had few reinforcements. In July, the Allies began to push them back. With better tanks, which had first been used in 1916, and the arrival of U.S. forces, the advance continued.

In November 1918, the German generals asked for peace rather than allowing the Allies to invade Germany. The other Central Powers had already admitted defeat. Bad harvests and blockades meant that many of their citizens faced starvation. At 11 a.m. on November 11, 1918, the fighting finally ceased.

In Their Own Words

"When 11 o'clock came [my companion] shut his watch up and said, 'I wonder what we are all going to do next!' To many of us it was practically the only life we had known. We had started so young."

Major Keith, Officer of the Australian Corps, recalls his reaction when the war ended

People in London celebrate the armistice that ended the fighting.

WHAT HAPPENED AFTER WORLD WAR I?

As the war ended, most of Europe was in chaos. Russia was in the middle of a civil war following the 1917 revolution. Revolutions also erupted in many other countries, including Germany, where Kaiser Wilhelm was forced from power on November 9, 1918. Even the victors, such as Britain and France, had to adjust to many changes and the loss of millions of young men in battle.

The leaders of France, Great Britain, and the United States meet at the Paris Peace Conference.

PEACE CONFERENCE

In 1919, leaders from the victorious nations met to discuss peace terms for the defeated Central Powers. The French and British believed Germany had caused the war by offering its unconditional support to Austria-Hungary in its dispute with Serbia. They wanted to ensure that the country could never threaten Europe again. The Treaty of Versailles was signed on June 28, 1919, and forced Germany to give up land to France, Poland, and elsewhere. Its army and navy were reduced to small defense forces, and its air force was banned altogether. The Germans also had to pay huge sums of money for the damage caused by the war in France and Belgium.

The peace **treaties** signed after the war made many other changes to the map of Europe and the wider world. The League of Nations was created to prevent future conflicts. However, even some of the victorious countries were unhappy with what was agreed. For example, Italy felt that the leaders of France, Great Britain, and the United States had ignored its claims for land.

The peace treaties created many new countries from old empires, such as Austria-Hungary.

President Woodrow Wilson (1856–1924)

Woodrow Wilson was the president who reluctantly took the United States into World War I. In early 1918, he set out 14 points that he thought should be part of any peace treaty. These included the right of all countries to govern themselves. He believed the League of Nations would prevent future wars, but he failed to persuade the U.S. Senate to support it. Without U.S. support, the League stood little chance of being successful.

END OF EMPIRES

The empires of Austria-Hungary and Turkey did not survive World War I. The peace treaties redrew the map of Eastern Europe. They created new countries such as Czechoslovakia (now the Czech Republic and Slovakia) and a reborn Poland. Disputes about the borders of these countries lasted for many decades.

New borders were also drawn in the Middle East, with Britain and France taking control of parts of the region. Arab leaders who had fought against the Turks were unhappy with the outcome, and the Middle East has continued to be the subject of arguments and conflict.

DISEASE SPREADS

The years after the war were hard for many people. An influenza epidemic—the Spanish Flu—killed more people than the war itself, including 550,000 people in the United States.

Spanish flu was partly spread by soldiers returning from the fighting.

LASTING PEACE?

Economic problems caused unemployment and poverty. The response in many countries was the rise of extreme **nationalist** leaders such as Italy's Mussolini and Germany's Hitler. In 1939, the world was at war again, as World War II began.

Adolf Hitler (1889–1945)

Adolf Hitler was born in Austria but joined the German army in 1914. Hitler believed that Germany had been betrayed by its generals and those who had signed the peace treaty. His desire for revenge was one of the causes of World War II.

In Their Own Words

"We shall have to fight another war all over again in 25 years."

David Lloyd-George, British prime minister on the Treaty of Versailles

....

"It cannot be that two million Germans should have fallen in vain. No, we do not pardon, we demand—vengeance!"

Adolf Hitler, who led Germany into World War II in 1939

Adolf Hitler (first from left with mustache) believed that Germany was shamed by surrendering to the Allies in 1918.

HOW DO WE REMEMBER WORLD WAR I?

The Great War, as it was called in 1918, caused the deaths of more people than any war before it. Millions more were wounded or scarred for life by their experiences.

Many of those who died are buried in huge cemeteries in northern France and Belgium. As the war stretched far beyond the Western Front, so did the long lists of names of soldiers killed in the fighting.

There are many memorials and ceremonies to remember World War I. In Australia and New Zealand, ANZAC day is commemorated on April 25, the day that ANZAC troops landed at Gallipoli. ANZAC Day was first held in 1916.

This war cemetery is home to the graves of Allied soldiers who died during the Gallipoli campaign.

VETERANS DAY

Every year on November 11, people across the world remember those who have been killed in wars. November 11 is the date of the end of World War I. At 11:00 a.m., the time when the guns fell silent, people remember those who died in that war and the many wars since then. In the United States, November 11 is called Veterans Day and is a national holiday honoring veterans from all wars. Veterans Day also reminds us that there are still people dying today in wars and conflicts around the world.

Military Deaths in World War I

Germany	⚰⚰⚰⚰⚰⚰⚰⚰⚰⚰⚰⚰⚰⚰⚰⚰⚰⚰⚰
Russia	⚰⚰⚰⚰⚰⚰⚰⚰⚰⚰⚰⚰⚰⚰⚰⚰⚰
France	⚰⚰⚰⚰⚰⚰⚰⚰⚰⚰⚰⚰⚰
Austria - Hungary	⚰⚰⚰⚰⚰⚰⚰⚰⚰
British Empire	⚰⚰⚰⚰⚰⚰⚰⚰
Italy	⚰⚰⚰⚰⚰
Turkey	⚰⚰⚰
United States	⚰
Others	⚰⚰⚰⚰⚰

⚰ = 100,000

This diagram shows the number of deaths suffered by each side during the war.

In Their Own Words

"Why do they never tell us that you are poor devils just like us, that your mothers are just as anxious as ours, and that we have the same fear of death—...forgive me comrade, how could you be my enemy?"

From Erich Maria Remarque's novel, All Quiet on the Western Front (1929). The words remind us that soldiers have much in common, even if they are fighting against each other.

TIMELINE

1914

June 28 — Gavrilo Princip kills Archduke Franz Ferdinand in Sarajevo. Austria-Hungary blames the Serbian government.

July 28– August 4 — War is declared, beginning with Austria-Hungary declaring war on Serbia and ending with Britain declaring war on Germany.

August 7 — British Expeditionary Force lands in France.

August 30 — Russian forces are defeated by Germany at the Battle of Tannenberg.

September 1–6 — First Battle of the Marne pushes German troops back from Paris. Trench warfare begins.

September 3 — HMS *Pathfinder* is sunk by a German U-boat, the first warship to be sunk in action by a submarine.

October 29 — Ottoman Empire (Turkey) enters the war on the side of Germany and Austria.

November — Trenches are established across the entire Western Front.

December 24 — German bomber aircraft attack Britain for the first time.

1915

April 25 — Allied forces land at Gallipoli in the Dardanelles.

May 23 — Italy enters the war on the Allied side.

October 6 — Serbia is finally invaded by the Central Powers, including Bulgaria, after resisting bravely since the start of the war.

November 19 — British forces advance on Baghdad, Mesopotamia (now Iraq).

1916

January 8 — Allied forces are evacuated from the Dardanelles.

February 21 — Battle of Verdun begins on the Western Front.

May 31 — The Battle of Jutland, the biggest naval battle of the war, begins in the North Sea.

June 4 — Russian army begins the Brusilov Offensive against Austria-Hungary, one of the most successful campaigns of the war.

| July 1 | Beginning of the Battle of the Somme, with 57,000 British troops killed or wounded on the first day. |
| September 15 | Tanks used for the first time during Battle of the Somme. |

1917
March 8	"February Revolution" begins in Russia, leading to the end of the reign of Tsar Nicholas II and to a new government in Russia.
March 26	Allied advance into Palestine begins.
April 6	United States declares war on Germany.
July 31	Battle of Passchendaele, also known as Third Battle of Ypres, begins.
October 24	Battle of Caporetto begins in northern Italy.
November 7	"October Revolution" begins in Russia, granting power to the Bolsheviks and marking the beginning of Soviet Russia.
December 9	Allied forces capture Jerusalem.

1918
March 3	Russia agrees to peace with Germany at Treaty of Brest-Litovsk.
March 21	German spring offensive begins, pushing Allied forces into retreat.
July 15	Second Battle of the Marne ends the German spring offensive.
September 12	U.S. forces attack St. Mihiel on the Western Front, the first U.S.-led offensive of the war.
September 15	Allied offensive from Salonika, Greece, begins.
November 11	Germany agrees to armistice with the Allies to end the war at 11:00 a.m. on the 11th day of the 11th month.
November 25	Last German forces surrender in East Africa.

After the war
| June 28, 1919 | Treaty of Versailles is signed, officially ending the war. |
| March 4, 1921 | U.S. Congress approves the burial of an unidentified World War I U.S. soldier in the Tomb of the Unknown Soldier in Washington, DC. |

GLOSSARY

alliance agreement between countries that they will help each other, such as when one of them is attacked by another country

Allies countries fighting together against the Central Powers, including the empires of France, Russia, and Great Britain, and later the United States

artillery heavy guns and cannons, usually moved around on wheels

Austria-Hungary former European monarchy made up of Austria, Hungary, and parts of other countries

blockade use of warships and other means to prevent supplies from reaching a country. Both sides in World War I tried to prevent food from reaching the other.

cavalry soldiers on horseback

Central Powers countries fighting against the Allies in World War I, including Germany, Austria-Hungary, and Turkey

civilian someone who is not a member of the armed forces

colony land that is ruled by people from another country

communist form of government in which all property is controlled by the government rather than individuals, and the government closely controls people's lives

convoy ships sailing together or escorted by warships to keep them safe from attack

Eastern Front border of the territory held by the Central Powers and the Allies, especially Russia, in the East

empire collection of colonies or provinces ruled from another country, such as the British Empire that covered large parts of the world in 1914

evacuate move people away from somewhere to keep them safe

infantry soldiers on foot

mobilize get soldiers or armies prepared and moved into position for war

nationalist person who is strongly in favor of their own country or wants their people to be independent of another country

offensive large attack using infantry, artillery, and other weapons

reinforcements additional forces arriving to assist in a battle

retreat move away from the enemy, usually because an army is losing a battle

revolution one form of government being replaced by another, often because of a violent uprising

stalemate situation where neither of two sides can win or gain an advantage

terrorist person who uses violence against civilians to achieve a particular goal

tonnage size or carrying capacity of a ship or fleet measured in tons

treaty agreement between two or more countries, for example to make peace at the end of a war

trench ditch dug by soldiers so they can shelter from enemy fire. Trenches were widespread in World War I, particularly on the Western Front, and trench systems became very complex.

truce agreement to stop fighting, often for only a short time

Western Front border of the territory held by the Central Powers and by the Allies in the West, where much of the fighting took place during World War I

FIND OUT MORE

BOOKS

Barber, Nicola. *Living Through World War I*. Chicago: Heinemann, 2012.

Price, Sean Stewart. *Yanks in World War I: Americans in the Trenches*. Chicago: Raintree, 2009.

Ross, Stewart. *World War I (Research It!)*. Chicago: Heinemann, 2010.

Yomtov, Nel. *True Stories of World War I*. Mankato, Minn.: Capstone, 2013.

WEB SITES

www.anzacday.org.au/history/ww1/ww1-00.html
The history of Australia's involvement in the war can be found on this website.

www.bbc.co.uk/schools/worldwarone/hq/activities.shtml
The BBC's World War I site for schools includes animations of poetry from the war.

www.firstworldwar.com
This site has a multimedia history of the war.

PLACES TO VISIT

National World War I Museum at Liberty Memorial, Kansas City, Missouri
www.theworldwar.org
Visit the museum to see permanent collections and exhibitions telling the story of World War I.

There are war memorials in thousands of towns and villages around the world. Visit your local memorial and look at the names of the young people who died in the war. You can also visit the Tomb of the Unknown Soldier at Arlington National Cemetery in Washington, DC.

TOPICS FOR FURTHER RESEARCH

- You may know about how World War I and other conflicts are remembered in your country, but what about the rest of the world?
- Find out about the weapons and technology that were used in the war. From tanks to heavy bombers, many military vehicles first appeared in World War I.
- Discover more about what conditions were like during the war, from life in the trenches to the experiences of those who served in the navies or flew aircraft behind enemy lines.

INDEX